PUZZLE
PYRAMID

Susannah Leigh
Illustrated by Brenda Haw

Contents

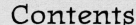
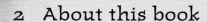

Edited by Jenny Tyler
Design Coordinator: Laura Parker

About this book

This book is about Fred and his adventure at a pyramid in Egypt. There is a puzzle on every double page. Solve them all and help Fred on his way. If you get stuck, the answers are on pages 31 and 32.

Fred has just finished a school project about Ancient Egypt.

Ancient Egypt

Fred

Ancient Egypt
By Fred, Class 3

The cobra goddess Wadjet was one of the pharaoh's protectors.

Pyramids

My Aunt Cleo has uncovered a pyramid, which lay buried underneath the Egyptian sand for thousands of years...

This is Fred's Aunt Cleo. She is an explorer and an archaeologist. She is in Egypt right now, working at the site of the pyramid she found. Cleo has written to Fred and told him all about her exciting discovery.

Aunt Cleo

Dear Fred,   Egypt, Saturday

It's been hard work, but the pyramid I discovered has almost been uncovered! The entrance is still buried under the sand, but I think I'm close to locating it. You must come and see for yourself. Catch the next flight to Cairo. Here's the ticket. I will meet your plane.

Love, Aunt Cleo xx

PS Bring your school project. It might be useful.

PPS I found a statue of a cobra near the pyramid. This could mean an Egyptian pharaoh is buried inside. There could even be hidden treasure! (I haven't found the jackal-headed god Anubis, though. He was the guardian of burial places. Help me find him when you get here...)

TICKET
PUZZLE AIR
ONE CHILD

My assistant Seth, the pyramid, me!

2

Things to spot

These objects are often found near Ancient Egyptian burial sites. Can you spot one on every double page? Remember what you've found. Some of them may be useful inside the pyramid.

collar

oil jug

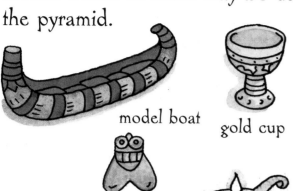

model boat

gold cup

precious stone

gold ring

lucky charm

golden fly

chisel

candle holder

scarab beetle brooch

shabti

casket

Meow!

Ancient Egyptians loved cats. See if you can spot a cat statue on every double page.

Sand pyramids

Someone's been busy building. Can you find at least one tiny pyramid hidden on every double page?

3

A sandy journey

Fred's plane landed in Egypt. Shading his eyes against the glare of the sun, Fred squinted in amazement at the mighty pyramid before him. It seemed hard to believe it had once been completely buried under the sand.

Fred couldn't wait to get a closer look. First he would have to find a way to the pyramid, but the sand was crumbling. He'd have to watch out for prickly palm trees, red ants, beetles and scorpions too. And where was Aunt Cleo? She had promised to meet him.

Can you find a safe way along the paths to the pyramid? Can you spot Aunt Cleo?

Cleo disappears

Fred reached the pyramid. He was about to call out to Aunt Cleo, who was climbing into a truck, when a tall man appeared at his side.

The man smiled, "I'm Seth, pyramid expert and Cleo's assistant. She's gone to the city to mail some letters. She asked me to look after you."

Swiftly, he marched Fred away from the pyramid, in the direction of Aunt Cleo's tent, where Fred was to stay.

Fred didn't understand. Hadn't Aunt Cleo promised to meet him? Then he spotted some things in the tent which made him wonder if Cleo had gone to the city at all.

What has Fred spotted?

Curious camels

Before Fred had time to say anything, Seth said, "There's no point in hanging around here. Take this money and go and buy some lunch in the village."

"I'd love to get a close-up view of the pyramid first," Fred suggested.

Seth shook his head quickly. "Out of bounds to children, I'm afraid," he smiled.

"Now find a camel and take a ride to the village. Bring me back a honey sandwich too."

Fred sighed. A camel ride did sound like fun. And Aunt Cleo would probably be back later. He could see plenty of camels, but which one should he take?

Which camel should Fred take today?

Lunch break

The camel ride was more uncomfortable than Fred had imagined. The camel's name was Abu. His owner, Bess, was very friendly.

"I'm off to buy some lunch," Fred told her.

"Mmm, that sounds like a good idea," Bess said. "I've got some money to spend too."

"Then let's have a picnic," smiled Fred, glad to have found a friend.

What can Fred and Bess buy to eat and drink, using all their money up?

I've got eighteen puzzle pennies. I'd like an ice cream. I'm really thirsty too. And I've got to buy Seth a honey sandwich.

I've got fifteen puzzle pennies. I'd like some fruit and some sweets. Oh, and something for Abu.

PRECIOUS OILS

MYRRH 8pp

CAMEL No.5 7pp

FRANKINCENSE 10pp

CUPCAKES 5pp EACH

HONEY SANDWICH 4pp EACH

BUNS 4pp EACH

FISH SANDWICH 2pp EACH

FIGS 9pp EACH

11

Fred is suspicious

The two new friends went back to the pyramid site. Bess tethered Abu and they walked over to the tent, chatting.

"My Aunt Cleo thinks the pyramid could be an important burial chamber, perhaps guarded by the god Anubis," Fred explained.

"Then there should be treasure inside!" Bess gasped.

Suddenly, Seth appeared.

Here's your sandwich. Is Aunt Cleo back?

Um... no.

Will you answer my questions about the pyramid? You said you were an expert.

Oh, all right.

Seth took them on a tour, telling them about the pyramid as they went. Fred listened carefully and flipped through his school project. He was sure Seth was lying.

What do you think?

Sandstorm

Suddenly, there was a huge rush of wind. The sand began to fly around them. Before Fred had time to think, he heard Bess cry, "Take cover – sandstorm!"

Fred dived behind the nearest rock and closed his eyes as the sand whirled around him.

BEFORE

When the storm cleared, Fred rubbed sand from his eyes. Several things had changed. And Fred saw something amazing revealed in the dunes before him. Something Aunt Cleo had asked him to look out for.

What things have changed?
What has Fred spotted?

AFTER

Captured

Fred was nose to nose with the statue of Anubis, guardian of burial chambers. This had to be the entrance to the pyramid, uncovered at last.

Suddenly, someone grabbed him – Seth! And at that moment, Fred knew for certain that Seth was up to no good.

Fred's mind whirled as Seth pushed him into a chamber and tied him up. Would he ever escape? Where was Bess? And where had he seen Amy and Geb before?

Do you recognize Amy and Geb? Is Bess here?

Cobra clue

Fred sat in the dark. Suddenly, he heard a scraping sound. Ghosts? Mummies? A head appeared. Bess! She wriggled through and untied Fred. Together they scrambled out of the chamber.

Crunch! A rockfall blocked the entrance. Now there was only one way to go – deeper into the pyramid.

"Perhaps we should look for a cobra," Fred suggested. "Aunt Cleo thought it marked the burial chamber, and that's surely where the treasure, and Seth, will be."

"It's lucky I've got a flashlight," Bess whispered.

Can you find the cobra and a way of getting to it?

Tricky hieroglyphs

At the end of a passage, Fred tried the door with the cobra picture. But it wouldn't open.

Bess shone her light on the wall in front of them. "Hieroglyphs," she hissed. She peered closer. "I think they show us how to open the door."

Fred looked at the little pictures carefully. "I recognize these objects," he cried. "I've been picking them up along the way!"

He whipped out his school project and turned to the chapter on picture messages. "I've found all the objects shown here, except one. Where is it?"

What does the picture message say? Can you spot the missing object?

Treasure!

Fred found the cobra statue at last and put it in place. As if by magic, the door of the tomb slowly creaked open. Fred and Bess gasped in surprise at what they saw inside. Treasure! There was a magnificent mummy case, wonderful paintings and lots of jewels, sparkling in a casket of solid gold.

"Aunt Cleo was right," Fred breathed. "The pyramid was hiding a burial chamber, and treasure too. We have to tell someone about this, before Seth gets here."

"I think we might be too late," Bess cried. "Look!"

What has Bess spotted?

23

The great escape

"I found a sneaky way in," Seth sneered. He jumped down while Geb blocked the door. Seth looked around the room. "Aha, treasure!" he grinned. "But first, to get rid of you two."

They had to escape. Suddenly Fred knew what to do. He would play a trick on Seth and pretend the mummy had come alive. He pointed to the casket behind Seth and yelled.

Seth whipped around in fright...

...quick as a flash, Fred and Bess dived under his legs and scrambled through the hole in the wall.

They were outside the pyramid now, looking down at the River Nile and – Aunt Cleo!

"Quick, into the boat," yelled Aunt Cleo.

But Fred and Bess were a long way up and the boat was a long way down. They would have to use the pyramid's rocky sides as steps to scramble down.

Can you find a safe way down to the boat?

River chase

They scrambled safely into the boat, but Seth and his gang had already found another boat and were escaping.

Quickly, Fred told Aunt Cleo what had happened inside the pyramid.

"We can't let Seth get away," Cleo said grimly.

"I know this river," Bess smiled.
"There are nests of crocodiles, strong net
fences and it's straight ahead to the police
boat. If we're clever and stay close behind,
Seth won't be able to turn around to get away."

Can you find the safe way to the police boat?

27

Celebration time!

Bess's plan was a success and Seth was captured before he knew it. A few days later, Fred, Bess and Aunt Cleo were at the City Museum, where the treasures of the pyramid were displayed.

"Seth wanted to steal the treasure," Cleo explained. "So Amy and Geb threw me into a truck and drove me to the desert. I escaped and was sailing to the pyramid site when I saw you. Thanks to your bravery, the treasure inside the pyramid has been revealed for everyone to enjoy."

"I don't think Seth's enjoying himself," Fred grinned.

Can you see what Seth is doing? (It's his punishment for trying to steal the pyramid treasure!)

I present you both with the fly of courage.

Well done!

Thank you, Mr. Mayor.

Wow, they are only awarded to the bravest Egyptians.

Pyramid puzzle

Later that evening, Fred and Bess sat on a rocky outcrop, sipping honey milkshakes and watching the sun set over the pyramid. Suddenly, Bess nudged Fred.

"Look at those tiny pyramids," she whispered.

"I wonder if there's any treasure hidden inside," Fred laughed.

You spotted the tiny pyramids, didn't you? But did you see who built them? Go back through the book and have a look.

Answers

pages 4-5

pages 6-7
Fred has spotted Aunt Cleo's wallet, her city bus pass, her bag and the letters Seth said she had gone to mail.

pages 8-9
Fred should take this camel. It is the only one going to the village today (Thursday).

pages 10-11
Fred buys a honey sandwich for 4pp, thirst quench juice for 5pp, a swirly cone for 9pp = 18pp.
Bess buys camel grass for 2pp, a bag of yummy sweets for 7pp, a pomegranate fruit for 6pp = 15pp.

pages 12-13
Seth is lying. Compare his information with the facts in Fred's school project.

pages 14-15
Fred has spotted the head of Anubis, the guardian of burial chambers.

pages 16-17
You have seen Amy and Geb on page 5. They were pulling Aunt Cleo toward a truck.

Bess is here.

pages 18-19

pages 20-21
The picture message says: To open the door, place these objects in any order on the table: shabti, model boat, cobra, collar, brooch, oil jug, chisel, gold ring, lucky charm.

Fred has found all the objects along the way, apart from the cobra. Here it is.

pages 22-23
Bess has
spotted
a foot.

pages
24-25

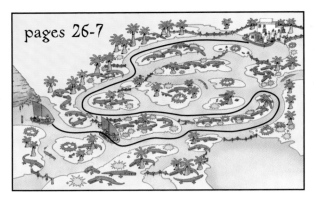
pages 26-7

pages 28-29
Seth, along with Amy
and Geb, are being
made to clean the
mummies.

page 30
The tiny pyramid
builders are mice.
They are hiding
on every
double
page.

Did you spot everything?

Burial site objects

collar — precious stone — golden fly — casket — oil jug — scarab beetle brooch — gold cup — model boat — chisel — lucky charm — gold ring — shabti — candle holder

Did you find a cat statue
and at least one tiny
pyramid, built by the
mice on every
double page?

The list below shows you which burial site
object is hidden on which page.

First published in 2004 by Usborne Publishing
Ltd., Usborne House, 83-85 Saffron Hill, London
EC1N 8RT, England.

www.usborne.com
Copyright © 2004 Usborne Publishing Ltd.

U.E. Printed in Portugal.